DIGITAL ADDICTION:

Breaking Free from the Shackles of the Internet, TV and Social Media

By:

Lora Ziebro

In the interest of full disclosure, this book contains affiliate links that might pay the author a commission upon any purchase from the company. While the author takes no responsibility for the business practices of these companies and or the performance of any product or service, the author or publisher has used the product or service and makes a recommendation in good faith based on that experience.

FOREWORD

When I first started reading "Digital Addiction" I was looking forward to finding good information that I could use with my own family. Like most, we have our struggles with the amount of 'screen time' that has slowly crept into our lives, and to be honest I'm probably the worst culprit. As a novelist born during the digital revolution I've developed writing habits that center on the cloud and it helps me stay productive because I can access my work no matter where the muse may happen to strike. But when I go back and check to see when I logged in and from where, it's shocking just how much of my books were written using my mobile phone or tablet. It makes me wonder how often my family or friends might have taken a backseat to me tapping away on a tiny screen. As a result, I began the book with the hope of finding some practical solutions and I'm happy to say that I was successful. I found quite a bit of information that was not only enlightening, it was also easy to apply in daily life. So simply based on that I felt that the book was a wonderful investment.

But what I had not counted on, was how the book exposed an almost eerily accurate prequel to my own work. In recent years I have written a great deal about the dangers of unrestricted technology and the potential risk we face of losing our humanity, or even our lives. The danger is very real and technological advancements of terrifying proportions are not as far off as we might think. "Digital Addictions" strikes directly to the heart of that issue and exposes many uncomfortable truths about how much of our lives we have slowly given over to electronic devices. It could easily be called a form of slavery and the author pulls no punches about the need to take a good long and honest look in the mirror.

So I hope you enjoy the book as much as I did, and with come away from it feeling as enriched and empowered as I did.

Jason Faris

Author of **"The Quantum Mechanic"** novel series

www.quantummechanicbook.com

Dedication

This book is dedicated to my sweetheart Tom, who has helped me find my vision with this book and who sneakingly began its inspiration. You are my love! And to my children- I want to be the best mom I can for you. I am forever blessed to be your mom. Lastly, this book is dedicated to every family trying to do it better and wanting freedom from distractions.

I want to thank Dave Figueroa, Jeff Gaines and Laurel Robinson for your help and insight with this book. Most importantly, I want to thank my Lord Jesus- without You, there'd be no me. You make me who and all that I am!

Table of Contents

Chapter 1: Are You a Digital Addict?

The definition of an addiction is: "The state of being enslaved to a habit or practice or to something that is psychologically or physically habit-forming, as narcotics, to such an extent that its cessation causes severe trauma"[1]. Drugs, alcohol, sex, gambling--these addictions are so destructive that most families will come to a place where they intervene and radically intrude in their loved ones way of living to help them find freedom from their addiction. Intrusion into someone's life is not something we normally do unless we feel there is a tremendous need and reason to do so. As a society, we let people live their lives, and as long as it doesn't affect us, we tend to mind our own business.

Are there acceptable addictions?

Anyone who has ever met, loved or known a person with an addiction can easily understand how destructive some addictions are. Despite this, there are some addictions that society deems socially acceptable. Smoking, for example, is one of these addictions. We understand as a society that smoking cigarettes greatly increases one's risk of getting cancer. Our government requires cigarette companies to place a health warning on the side of cigarette boxes. For the most part though, it has become an acceptable addiction. It is an addiction that we don't intervene with, unless of course, cancer or emphysema starts to show. Only then, families will find themselves doing and saying the hard things to help or encourage

---

[1] http://www.dictionary.com/browse/addiction?s=t

their loved one to quit smoking and hopefully extend their life.

It took a long time for the effects and dangers of smoking to really be understood. There was a lot of medical evidence that had to be revealed in order to show people the possible dangers that long term smoking caused on the body, in order for them to accept that smoking was dangerous. Even still, with all the evidence and warnings, smoking is still an acceptable addiction. But this is not a book about the harmfulness of smoking- that road was traveled long ago when the warning signs were first appearing. This book is about the dangers of a seemingly new addiction- a Digital Addiction.

We exist with and are surrounded by a digital world. Every day we see advancements- applications and platforms are being invented faster than we can imagine. These advancements are birthing a new way of living, and with it, a new addiction. Like smoking, this addiction is acceptable, multi-generational and everywhere in our modern culture. It is even in places you wouldn't think to find a problem. We as a society have yet to fully realize or understand the effects of digital addiction.

What is Digital addiction? Digital addiction (DA) is simply an addiction to electronics and digital media. It deals with everything from television to texting. In many ways, this dependence on digital media is relatively new and almost completely untreated by the medical community. There are countries like China that are leading the way in diagnosing and treating DA, but it is almost unheard of in America. In this book I will highlight what I believe is a growing concern in this country. My hope is that once the personal awareness of a problem exists, individual steps can be taken to balance and establish healthy digital media use.

What caused me to write this book?

The other day I was in a restaurant with my family waiting to be seated. We have a larger family (5 kids), so this can usually take some time. I am analytical by nature so I found myself observing people during our wait. As I looked around, I was shocked and saddened by how little personal, intimate inter-action I observed going on between family members. There was almost no eye contact, no real conversations and nothing that would deepen their relationships. There were countless families where every member seemed to be using a gadget--except maybe the youngest, who was being overlooked and using that time to get into trouble to get some attention. More and more I see this problem. There is so much at our hands and so little in our relationships! Things that are real and meaningful are being replaced by things that are short and trivial. This is an epidemic in this country and one that we must fight against! It is time for intervention.

Now, lest you think I am being too dramatic, I cannot tell you how many times I have spoken to kids, preteens and teens who tell me that it is completely normal to text their friend that they are physically hanging out with, instead of talking to them. Did you catch what I just said? They are texting each other in lieu of talking face to face even though they are in the same room. I have also witnessed and known of parents Facebooking, emailing and texting their own children instead of talking directly to them. This is a problem.

I can personally admit that there are times I am on a device of some sort while my kids are near me and time and life are lit-erally just flying by around me. When I'm done, I'm shocked by how much time I spent "away" from them, even though I am in the same room. Have you ever found this true of you?

If we are not careful, we can easily spend most of our waking hours sitting in front of a television, computer, smartphone or other device, or gaming. It is no surprise for children to get caught up in these distractions, but parents should lead them and teach them self-discipline. They can do that by first setting the right example in their own lives. The purpose of this book is to point out some of our many digital distractions and what can be done as a parent, spouse, or friend to recapture the joys of a simplified life. This book has four primary goals:

1. To isolate areas in your life so that you can evaluate if change is necessary.

2. To correct bad habits, thoughts or ideas.

3. To instruct you in how to change and better use your time.

4. To encourage you for the road ahead.

This book is for the person who realizes that a change is necessary. If you are reading it, good for you! This means that you already are aware that things have to change.

Chapter 2: TV

There is no better place to start this book than the topic of TV. Before smartphones, tablets, video games, and the Internet, there was TV. TV watching in this country is a problem. An article in the NY Daily News on Sept 19, 2012, reported that Americans spend 34 hours a week watching TV, according to Nielsen numbers.[2] If 34 hours does not seem that bad to you, consider that there are only 168 hours in a week and most people sleep an average of 6.8 hours of sleep a night. That leaves about 120 hours of time awake.[3] That's about one quarter of your total weekly awake time that is spent watching television. That number is shocking!

Now I'm not going to swing the pendulum too far to one side and say that watching any television is bad. We all watch television from time to time. Nothing is wrong with watching a good movie, keeping up with a favorite show, or catching up on the news. The problem is the **amount** of time that we spend in front of the TV. When television consumes 34 hours a week of our precious time, then we have to do something we don't like to do freely – limit ourselves!

The bottom line is that if we spend too many hours in front of the TV, many times those are precious hours taken away from our families. I say "many times" because there are a lot of families who watch good wholesome shows <u>together</u> and actually

---

[2] http://www.nydailynews.com/entertainment/tv-movies/americans-spend-34-hours-week-watching-tv-nielsen-numbers-article-1.1162285#ixzz33pIV9Ylc

[3] http://www.gallup.com/poll/166553/less-recommended-amount-sleep.aspx

spend time <u>together</u> as they watch the shows. They also limit their overall TV viewing.

Consider your TV watching patterns. Do you:

1. Watch television in one room while other family members watch in separate rooms?

2. Have no contact or interaction during television viewing?

3. Merely spend too many hours in front of the television?

4. If any of these are true of you, I must ask you:

What would your home like look like if those hours devoted to the television, were instead devoted to your family?

What if, instead of watching television in isolation from your family, you devoted that time to building, healing, loving, preserving and restoring the relationships of those around you? Relationships can be hard, but they don't get better when they are ignored. I wonder what <u>all</u> American families would look like if we spent those same television viewing hours--34 hours a week-- in purposeful time with our families.

So ask yourself, how much TV do you watch each day? Are you one of those people who spend 34 hours a week or more in front of the television? Maybe you are thinking your TV habits are not that bad? Let's see. I'll break down some numbers to get a full picture of what this amount of TV viewing really equates to.

If you <u>only</u> watch prime time TV (8 – 10 P.M.) that is 2 hours a day x 7 days and that gives you 14 hours of viewing time a week. That's 56 hours a month (**2.5 full days of TV viewing**) and 672 hours a year (**28 full days of TV**). However, most people watch shows before and after prime time. If you add in the weekends or additional television viewing during your favorite sports' seasons, you can see how easily you will blow past those previous numbers. So let's calculate the following numbers- If you watch TV between 7 and11 P.M.--1 hour before and after prime time--that is 4 hours a day. If you also watch more TV on weekends, (8 hours, conservatively) then you are watching 36 hours a week and 136 hours a month. **That is a little over 5 full days of TV viewing a month**. If you multiply that by 12 months **you are watching 1,632 hours of TV a year – 64 full days of TV**! Wouldn't you agree that those numbers are alarming? Those are precious hours taken away from building lasting relationships with the people you love.

Recognizing the need for change is always the first step to change, no matter what the issue is. Obviously, you won't be able to change your habits overnight. As with anything else, it is a process.

If you do realize there is a problem with how much TV you are watching, how can you change? Here are some suggestions to get you on the right course. These are just different ways of achieving the same outcome – less time lost to the TV. I will be breaking down the time saved by choosing one of these options, **based on the average of watching TV for 34 hours a week (1,768 hours a year)**.

Regaining Time Stolen by TV

Idea 1 - Stick to Prime Time. If you normally watch TV several hours a day, start by cutting your viewing time in half and maybe allow yourself a little more viewing time on a week-end. So if you normally watch 4 hours and cut it down to 2, **you will regain 14 hours a week, 56 hours a month and 672 hours a year.**

Idea 2 - Only watch your favorite show(s). Limit TV viewing to just one (or two) favorite shows a night. I'm sure you can admit that sometimes you are just watching reruns of shows or watching shows just to pass the time while you wait for your favorite shows to start anyway. This is really something to consider: **how much time do you spend watching things you don't even want to watch or have already seen before, while you wait for your favorite shows?** If your favorite show (on the higher end) is an hour long, **you will be cutting out 3 hours a day of TV. You will regain 21 hours a week, 90 hours a month and a whopping total of 1,080 hours a year.** Another way to think about why you should follow this method is that you are spending 1,008 hours a year on shows you don't really want to watch. That's a whole lot of time wasted on something you don't even enjoy!

Idea 3 - Limit your television time so it's not daily but just on specific days. If you watch on average 4 hours of television a day, **just by cutting out one day of TV watching a week, you are regaining a total of 192 hours a year.** All that time gained that can be directed to something far more important. Now imagine how much time you can save and re-gained if you just cut out TV watching each day?

Idea 4 - Limit your TV time to weekends. If you cut out watching TV during the week and just watch it selectively (no more than 4 hours a day) on Fridays, Saturdays and Sundays, **you will be regaining 768 hours a year**. I personally feel that the weekend is when the best shows are on anyway. This is pretty much what we do in our home. I'm about making memories, and we make TV viewing a "memory moment." We all get together, grab some popcorn and blankets, and enjoy our time together while we watch a good movie or show.

Idea 5 - Set your own goal. Begin by calculating how much TV you watch per day/year and then set a goal of how much you want to decrease it by. For example, say you want to **re-gain** 500 hours a year from viewing TV, you would have 41.6 hours of viewing time a month which breaks down to approximately 1 ½ hours a day or 9 hours a week that you can split up however you see fit.

Is TV a waste of time? It can be. **If it is taking you away from realizing your dreams, completing your tasks, or fulfilling your responsibilities, then yes, it is a waste of your time!**

Changing this behavior won't be easy and it will demand a lot of patience and perseverance on your part. However, greater discipline in this area is certainly worth your time and effort.

Here is an example of **what you could achieve** if you used those hours more wisely, <u>based on the 1,536 hours a year in average spent on television</u>:

- **Pilot** - Under Federal Aviation Regulations, you need a minimum of 30 hours for a recreational pilot certificate, and 40 hours for a private pilot certificate. Among the requirements for a commercial Pilot's certificate in the USA is a minimum of 250 hours of flight time. [4]

- **EMT** - EMTs usually complete a course that is about 120-150 hours in length.

---

4 http://www.flightsimaviation.com/data/FARS/part_61.html

- **Paramedic** - Paramedic courses can be between 1,200 to 1,800 hours.[5]

- **Massage Therapist-** The time it takes to become a massage therapist varies, but at least 500 hours are required from most massage schools.[6]

- **Write a manuscript or novel** - It can take as little as 3 months to a year to write a manuscript or novel, depending on daily time devoted to writing.[7]

- **Get in shape** - ½ - 1 hour of exercise a day, combined with a nutritious diet will help transform your health and get you in better shape, no matter what your current fitness level is. Taking the time regained from cutting out TV and transferring it into physical activity will create a better, stronger, healthier you!

- **Further your education:**

  For an Associate's Degree you need between 60-80 credit hours, depending on your major.

  For a Bachelor's Degree you need between 120 and 150 hours, depending on your major.

(Note that credit hours are not the same time as literal hours. Three credit hours means one semester taking a 3-credit

---

5 https://www.cpc.mednet.ucla.edu/node/27

6 https://www.amtamassage.org/findamassage/credential.html

7 http://www.goodreads.com/topic/show/1248373-how-long-does-it-take-you-to-write-a-book

course. Still, by taking online courses instead of watching TV you can find yourself getting a diploma a lot sooner than you think!)

- **Become a better parent, spouse, child, friend** – This can begin with just 1 hour of purposeful and direct time spent each day with those we love. It can be further achieved by taking any of those hours spent watching television and purposefully applying them to the nurture, care and growth of those who love us and need us the most. Unlike television, by doing this you are building a legacy that will pass on to future generations.

Not only should we monitor how much time we spend watching television, but care needs to be taken with the content of what we view.

The why of filtering television

Our children's development should be one of our first priorities as parents. We should be purposeful with not just their physical and intellectual development, but also their emotional and spiritual growth. Violent shows and movies; negative news; or programs that promote drugs, drinking, premarital sex or extramarital affairs, abuse/disrespect of women, disrespect of parents, or emasculation of men--these shows have an effect on our children! Filtering and parental guidance is a must in this area.

The American Academy of Pediatrics has discussed these concerns for a long time, stating in 2013 "For nearly 3 decades,

the AAP has expressed concerns about the amount of time that children and teenagers spend with media and about **some of the content they view**. In a series of policy statements, **the AAP has delineated its concerns about media violence, sex in the media, substance use, music and music videos, obesity and the media, and infant media use.**"[8]

In reference to the effect of violence on children: "Teenagers who spend a lot of time playing violent video games or watching violent shows on television have been found to be more aggressive and more likely to fight with their peers and argue with their teachers, according to a study in the Journal of Youth and Adolescence."[9]

"The typical American child will view more than 200,000 acts of violence, including more than 16,000 murders, before age 18. Television programs display 812 violent acts per hour; children's programming, particularly cartoons, displays up to 20 violent acts hourly."[10]

"Additionally, **children who watch televised violence are desensitized to it. They may come to see violence as a fact of life and, over time, lose their ability to empathize with both the victim and the victimizer.**"[11]

---

8 http://pediatrics.aappublications.org/content/132/5/958.full

9 http://mobile.nytimes.com/blogs/well/2015/07/06/screen-addiction-is-taking-a-toll-on-children/

10 http://www.aacap.org/aacap/medical_students_and_residents/mentorship_matters/developmentor/the_impact_of_media_violence_on_children_and_adolescents_opportunities_for_clinical_interventions.aspx

11

http://www.aacap.org/aacap/medical_students_and_residents/mentorshi

"While the causes of youth violence are multifactorial and include such variables as poverty, family psychopathology, child abuse, exposure to domestic and community violence, substance abuse and other psychiatric disorders, **the research literature is quite compelling that children's exposure to media violence plays an important role in the etiology of violent behavior.** While it is difficult to determine which children who have experienced televised violence are at greatest risk, there appears to be a strong correlation between media violence and aggressive behavior within vulnerable "at risk" segments of youth."[12]

A lot of television programs, movies and video games today seem to diminish, or outright remove, the gravity and negative consequences of violence, abuse, and law breaking. It seems especially true of shows targeted to the younger generations (adolescent to young adult). I find that these programs don't just remove the negative consequences, but they seem to glorify wrong behaviors. This can be very confusing and damaging for young people trying to learn the differences between right and wrong. When you tell your child that something is wrong, but they are viewing programs that promote and celebrate that behavior, there is bound to be confusion.

The concern isn't just limited to our children. Television has a way of affecting adults too! It has the ability to affect our

p_matters/developmentor/the_impact_of_media_violence_on_children_an d_adolescents_opportunities_for_clinical_interventions.aspx

12
http://www.aacap.org/aacap/Medical_Students_and_Residents/Mentorsh ip_Matters/DevelopMentor/The_Impact_of_Media_Violence_on_Children_a nd_Adolescents_Opportunities_for_Clinical_Interventions.aspx

moods and actions. It can also be a substantial influence on how we view and handle life, relationships, love, marriage, God, morality, etc.

For example, it is very hard for a man or woman to compete with the false and unrealistic images of the "perfect body" or "perfect marriage/relationship" fed to us in movies and television. Due to these unrealistic images, I have had to remind many people I know that we should not use movies and celebrity relationships as a personal standard for our own life-- especially considering that most of Hollywood can't stay married, faithful or committed for very long. Think about it...why seek relationship advice from people who are chronically in unhealthy relationships? If someone doesn't know how to love properly and be committed, he or she is the wrong person for us to mirror our own relationships after. So don't view your own life through their eyes. That deals not only with the act of love, but who to love, how to love, why to love and what love is. When all is said and done, any couple with any sort of longevity in a relationship or marriage will admit that the visions of "love" seen in most Hollywood movies and television shows are far removed from the true, deep commitment and choice that real love requires. Love is a choice, lust is a desire.

You might think I'm being too dramatic, so I'm going to give you a personal example from a group of people I know. Several years ago a show came out that celebrated adultery. We knew a couple that lived on a block where all the married women would get together every week to watch the show. In an unusually short period of time, almost all of the same women on this block were divorced, and most because of adulterous affairs. I believe that watching the show had a two-fold effect: 1. It gave the women a desire to cheat on their spouse and 2. Made them dissatisfied with their husbands because of how the "ideal" man was portrayed in the show. Naturally, their husbands couldn't compete with these images of love because they were grossly misrepresented. The show glorified acts of adultery and lust but failed to show the absolute ruin and brokenness that comes from these actions. I've seen the same thing happen with women feeling dissatisfaction in their own marriage after reading romance novels, or men who view pornography being displeased with the way their wife looks. What you watch can have a huge impact on your personal relationships.

I wonder how many relationships are ruined by people confusing lust with love.

From now on, when scrolling through the channels to make a decision as to what you will watch and how much time you will dedicate to watching TV, remember the negative effects some shows can have on you personally. Here are a few things to think about or ask yourself before you choose what to watch on television/movie:

Ask yourself...

- What effect on your children or marriage would there be by viewing this show?

- Is it an unfair or unbalanced portrayal of life?

- Does it promote unrealistic expectations that will leave you unsatisfied?

- Does this dissatisfaction leave you unhappy and will it negatively affect your marriage, relationships with your children or with people at work?

- Does this show make you desire wrong things?

21

- Does it tempt you to violence, crime or harm?

- How will viewing this show profit and/or benefit you?

If you find you answered affirmatively to some of these questions and see the importance for change, here are some ideas to help you change.

- **Idea 1** - When you recognize that you are being affected by a show in a negative way, flip the channel to something more profitable and/or positive. It's a simple idea, but it's effective.

- **Idea 2** - Filter what you watch. Identify what triggers wrong thoughts, feelings and emotions. Filter your shows by that content, and avoid watching those shows.

- **Idea 3** – Limit your exposure to the news. As a whole, what is reported in the news is negative in nature and can cause feelings of anger, despair, depression, anxiety and fear. If you have a sensitive conscience, viewing all that negativity can overwhelm you. Instead consider viewing programs that depict acts of courage, kindness, goodness and inventiveness. If you are going to watch the news, watch reports that positively affect you or inspire you towards greater things.

- **Idea 4** – Fill your time with something better. Realize that watching television is nothing more than an act of entertainment that is usually done to overcome boredom. Fill your time with something better--a hobby, a good book, exercise, learn or gain new skills, start a new business, embark on a new career or build stronger relationships with those around you. Find another, more profitable way to entertain yourself. **Television is not the only way to avoid boredom.** If you follow my strategies for limiting TV viewing time, you can follow that dream that you've always wanted to achieve and start taking steps to fulfill it.

The ideas I gave you were just to get you thinking. **There are a lot of other things you can be doing, which will bring you much more fulfillment.**

Chapter 3: Social Media – The Internet's Social Gathering Spot

Remember being young, in school, and looking for places to go with friends to do nothing more than just hang out? It was great finding a place where we all could go and get together to know each other deeper than we had in school. We would look to find people to share our lives with; people who accepted us as we were; people with whom we could just be ourselves. Sometimes those days were difficult and sometimes those days were our greatest childhood moments. In some respects, social media is the equivalent of that for young people today. Kids still get together in person, but for a large part, social media has caused a shift to a digital or Internet social gathering spot.

Unlike most of us who had to search for places to hang out when we were younger, social media affords young people the ability to be "with" each other without finding a place to go and without curfew limits. There are positives and negatives to having this ability. The biggest concern with social media is the sheer amount of time that people spend on it. There are so many different social media platforms and new ones seem to pop up daily--all of them looking to be the next "hang out place." There are enough social gathering spots to get lost in for hours. This is true for kids and adults. Hours of our lives can literally be lost looking at sites like Facebook, Pinterest, Twitter, YouTube, etc. Unlike going home from your friend's house and spending the rest of the time with your family where the parent-child relationship can be built, social media keeps children and parents largely separate even though they are in the home at the same time. There is no "going home from your friend's house," there is only the constantly available digital gathering place.

There also seems to be a shift in how kids communicate with each other. As I said earlier, now when kids get together, many times their relationship still centers on the digital platforms. This is especially true with the use of smartphones.

"The vast majority of teens (95%) spend time with their friends outside of school, in person, at least occasionally. But for most teens, this is not an everyday occurrence. Just 25% of teens spend time with friends in person (outside of school) on a daily basis."[13]

There is no limit to the amount of time you can spend on the Internet. There is a famous quote largely attributed to Albert Einstein that says, "I fear the day technology will surpass our human interaction. The world will have a generation of idiots." I don't think we'll have a generation of idiots but I fear we will have a generation void of what defines us the most as humans – relationship.

The why of problems with excessive Internet/social media use

There are real reasons why this should matter to everyone. The younger generations whose understanding of life is developed in the formative years are being raised and built on a lifestyle of partial isolation due to digital addiction. Living in isolation is not the way human beings were meant to exist with each other. We were meant to live life in a community. While we are technically still in a community, it is in some respects merely an illusion of a community since the most basic elements of human contact are removed when individuals are

---

13 http://www.pewInternet.org/2015/08/06/teens-technology-and-friendships/

engaged in digital amusements rather than meaningful face-to-face communication.

In addition to isolation, there is another problem with social media. There is this unique separation from human responsibility or intrinsic morality that is fostered by many forms of social media. It can be very disturbing. There are children telling other children to kill themselves or harm themselves; there are people embracing, celebrating and seeking to engage in fights, knockouts, rapes, violence, and crime. Additionally, with the propensity to record everything, there is a troubling distancing of social responsibility, separating people from their natural duty to help another human in trouble in lieu of the ability to record the event.

It's not just about children. Unlike the past where the newest fad was mostly embraced by the younger generations, the Internet is cross generational. This is an issue because everyone is being affected by it--moms, dads, grandparents, siblings, children, friends, and neighbors. Time spent surfing the web, and time spent away from person-to-person social interaction is increasing and is affecting the building of personal relationships. The social addiction in this country is alarming. You cannot go anywhere without seeing people "connected" to the Internet. We have yet to see or understand the full effects of this because this is the first time in the history of the human race that something has so significantly come between the normal building of interpersonal relationships and normal peer/familial community bonding.

Studies are being done in an attempt to understand the effects on Internet use and relationships. In a paper entitled "Adolescent Screen Time and Attachment to Parents and Peers," released by the Archives of Pediatrics and Adolescent Medicine, the authors suggest a correlation, stating: "The more screen exposure teenagers get, the more detached they are from those around them."[14]

In another study conducted in New Zealand in 2004, researchers found that there "was a **4 or 5 percent increase in detachment to parents for every hour spent watching TV or surfing the Web**, respectively. It's not all about the parents, either— "**more time spent gaming was associated with low attachment to peers as well**." Conversely, "**More time spent reading offline and doing homework was associated with higher attachment to parents**." In addressing the rise in detachment to parents and peers the authors note that, "It is also possible that adolescents with poor attachment relationships with immediate friends and family use screen-based activities to facilitate new attachment figures such as online friendships or parasocial relationships with television characters or personalities." For those children who do struggle making friends, the Internet can be a place where they can find others like them and a place to go where they can be accepted by others who identify with their struggles.

While the Internet has become a social gathering spot and "connected" many people virtually, people as a whole are "also more lonely and distant from one another in their unplugged lives...not only changing the way we interact online, **it's straining our personal relationships, as well**", says social psychologist Dr. Sherry Turkle, from the Massachusetts Institute of Technology.

Dr. Turkle's book Alone Together (Basic Books, 2011) examines the effect social media and texting have on our culture and relationships. She discusses how this lack of intimacy can cause problems in relationships: "Children say they try to

---

[14] http://arstechnica.com/gadgets/2010/03/increased-Internet-tv-time-correlated-to-teen-detachment/

make eye contact with their parents and are frustrated because their parents are looking down at their smartphones when they come out of school or after school activities. Young men talk about how only a few years ago, their dads used to watch Sunday sports with them and during the station breaks or between plays, they used to chat. Now their fathers are too often checking their email during games."[15]

Additionally she says "the most dramatic change is our ability to be "elsewhere" at any point in time, to sidestep what is difficult in a personal interaction and go to another place where it does not have to be dealt with."[16] So in the past where a person had to learn to cope with uncomfortable situations and find a way to adapt, learn, and grow from them, now people can and do retreat to their digital world and bypass that experience. They are "there" and "gone" at the same time.

Another thing to consider is the quality of relationships we make on these sites. The friendships we have through social media are many times not real friendships in the way we used to count friendships. Dr. Turkle states that while we have a lot of "friends" online, they can "be more like 'fans' than friends". Our relationships with them "can sustain us and distract us and make it less likely for us to look beyond them to other social encounters. They can provide the illusion of companionship without the demands of friendship, without the demands of intimacy."[17]

There are a lot of benefits to using social media, and culturally it is an important means of communication in this modern

---

[15] http://www.apa.org/monitor/2011/06/social-networking.aspx

[16] Ibid.

[17] Ibid.

age. Every family is different and unique. In the same way, how social media affects each family will be different. There will be both positive and negative effects of social media usage in the family dynamic. Ultimately, it is essential that you have a personal awareness of the fact that social media can have a negative effect on your family and that you know how to prevent it from being a problem in your own home.

Negative effects from or associated with social media/media

- Time away from family unit.

- Media use is not without consequence on physical health. Studies find that high levels of media use are associated with academic problems, problems with sleep, unhealthy eating, and more. The American Academy of Pediatrics (AAP) recommends that adolescents have less than two hours of screen time per day.[18]

- In an exploratory study done in China, evidence showed that there is a reasonable association linking self-injury and Internet addiction. "The correlation between Internet addiction and self-injury was very high; Internet addicts were about 2.5 times more likely to have engaged in at least some form of self-injury in the past six months."[19]

- Forty-two percent of social media-using teens have had someone post things on social media about them

---

[18] http://www.hhs.gov/ash/oah/news/e-updates/eupdate-nov-2013.html

[19] http://arstechnica.com/science/2009/12/Internet-addicted-youth-engage-in-other-forms-of-self-injury/

that they cannot change or control.20

- Twenty-one percent of teen social media users report feeling worse about their own life because of what they see from other friends on social media.21

- Experts worry that this digital interaction is making it harder for teens to:

  1. Build relationships

  2. Develop essential social skills

  3. Know how to manage person-to-person interaction with someone

- A lot of bad, misleading, biased information is learned and spread across social media and the Internet in general. This is across the board from science, to history, to politics, to sex and to religion. If you are not careful, you or your children can be consuming misinformation and spreading it.

- Making poor decisions without realizing their long term effects – e.g. sexting, sending/sharing nude photos on web or through texts; posts that are criminal in nature or threatening; posts that can affect careers, school admissions, healthy relationships, etc.

---

[20] http://www.pewInternet.org/2015/08/06/teens-technology-and-friendships/

[21] http://www.pewInternet.org/2015/08/06/teens-technology-and-friendships/

- The pain and difficulty of being bullied is almost inescapable now because of the ability to cyber bully. Combine that with the global platform that social media has and it's easy to see how far-reaching cyber bullying can be. In the past, kids could retreat to their home as a safe haven. Now, with the Internet and smartphones, cyber bullying can come into a child's home and leave them vulnerable to the constant bullying of their peers.

- Parents can't always police. No matter how much you try, you can easily find yourself out of the loop when it comes to what your children are doing on social media. This may be a shock to some parents, but there are apps that help a child trick and deceive their parents. Whether that was the app creator's original intention or not is beside the point. The fact is that some apps can be used to mask or hide online activity. As a parent, you should carefully monitor what apps your child has or be the one in control of downloading any new apps. Don't think that because you look at your phone statement sheets, you will have an idea what your kids are doing. Phones don't track what apps your children are on or what they do. And unless you know what you're looking for, you may miss it altogether. Before you allow an app to be installed you should research it, be aware of its abilities, consider how it can be used outside of the primary use and look at its reviews.

- Additionally, there are lots of ways children can get onto sites that are dangerous or unhealthy for them. Pornography is easily accessible online and is known to have a damaging, long term effect on a lot of men and women. I know families that require a buddy system for online usage. There is accountability in a buddy system. There are several great filtering systems to help prevent accidental and purposeful visits to harmful or pornographic websites. In our home, we use Safe Eyes which is downloaded on our computer, devices and phone. There are several choices available for the devices that you may have.

- One in four children in chat rooms on the Internet will be solicited by a child predator.[22] Pedophiles and people looking to take advantage of young impressionable minds are a very real threat on the Internet. Be aware of your child's activity online. While you don't want to make your child fearful in regards to the Internet, letting them know the dangers online and giving them tools to make wise decisions is a prudent step. Consider that 70 % of children "friend" someone even if they don't know them. That's a big number. Special Agent Greg Wing of the FBI cyber squad says, **"It's an unfortunate fact of life that pedophiles are everywhere online.**"[23]

Positive effects of social media use:

- Health professionals can use media to promote people's health. TV shows can share important information on various health topics. Mobile technology presents ever-new opportunities for delivering health interventions, such as reminders for physical activity or tobacco quitting tips.[24]

- It increases cultural awareness. People have a greater

---

[22] http://drphil.com/articles/article/166

[23] https://www.fbi.gov/news/stories/2011/may/predators_051711

[24] http://www.hhs.gov/ash/oah/news/e-updates/eupdate-nov-2013.html

understanding of other cultures and also have a larger global reach because of the access that the web allows. It is not unheard of for people to have and maintain multiple relationships with people all over the world. The Internet provides various ways for people who are separated by long distances, to be able to keep in contact with each other. This can be accomplished by viewing pictures, following someone's status, emailing, or talking audibly or visually to one another.

- It does not require that children leave their house in order to connect with their peers. Whether they are connecting through chat rooms, forums, boards, instant messenger or virtual worlds, the digital arena affords a greater ability to communicate with each other, all within the safety of the home.

- With the right tools and rules in place, parents can use the Internet as a great way to teach and guide their children through the many "social" learning experiences that the Internet provides. It's a great way for parents to be involved in their children's' circle of peers and aware of what's going on in their social world. Having that window into your child's world can also help you better navigate your own relationship with them.

- It provides access to education. Whether you want to learn something for school or for your own interests, the web is an excellent place to go build knowledge. (Just check your sources and make sure you are getting accurate information!)

- The ability to find peers. The opposite of cyber bullying is the ability to find peers who understand, accept and relate to you. They might not even be in your school or your state. The Internet opens the doors to friendships and support that you or your child might not get locally.

- It opens a world of creativity. There are so many different ways that the Internet aids in creativity. It is a place of learning, exploring, taking part in some type of art form/medium, creative expression through blogs, websites, YouTube, graphic design, etc. A creative mind may find the Internet to be a great place to develop, hone and explore creative avenues.

- Making money. I could write a whole book on making money on the Internet. Thankfully my husband covered this in his book so I don't have to. Be sure to read "Building Wealth through Income Streams: Mindset. Motivation. Mastery". I'll just say this to sum it up: if you have access to the Internet, have a heartbeat, and are willing to put in some time, you can make money on the Internet.

How much time are we talking about?

Many countries, including America, consider the compulsive use of the Internet to be an emerging mental health issue. They are seeing the addictive nature of compulsive internet use and are studying its effects but there is still so much unknown about excessive digital use. China was one of the first to put a label on "Internet Addiction" and consider it a clinical disorder. Not only do they call internet addiction a clinical disorder but they have rehabilitation centers like Daxing Boot Camp (**Daxing Internet Addiction Treatment Centre**) set up to help people struggling with it.

Tao Ran, a psychiatrist and colonel in the People's Liberation Army stated 'Internet addiction leads to problems in the brain similar to those derived from heroin consumption, but, generally, it is even more damaging. It destroys relationships and deteriorates the body without the person knowing. All of them have eyesight and back problems and suffer from eating disorders. In addition, we have discovered that their brain capacity is reduced by eight per cent, and the psychological afflictions are serious. If someone is spending six hours or more on the internet, we consider that to be an addiction.' Not everyone agrees with the idea that the symptoms of excessive digital use as similar to substance addiction. Some doctors "believe internet addiction should be considered a social deviation, and not a medically 'curable' condition."

There are different groups that have tried to track and compile how much time teens are actually spending on social media or media in general each year; however, it is really hard to gauge or to break down that number exactly. The surveys below discuss media usage as a whole and specifically as it deals with the Internet. When we are discussing time spent on media usage, we are specifically talking about time spent watching television, using a device like a tablet (including smartphones), and time spent on the computer (except for in-school use). The time breakdowns below do not include texting and talking on the phone.

According to some more recent surveys:

"The average 8 to 10-year-old spends nearly eight hours a day with a variety of different media, and older children and teenagers spend more than 11 hours per day...Young people now spend more time with media than they do in school—it is the leading activity for children and teenagers other than sleeping."[25]

"Today's **teens spend more than 7.5 hours a day consuming media** — watching TV, listening to music, surfing the Web, social networking, and playing video games, according to a 2010 study of 8 to 18 year olds conducted by the Kaiser Family Foundation. The study also found a particular rise in time spent on mobile devices and an overall increase of about an hour and 20 minutes since 1999."[26]

Conversely, "According to the Bureau of Labor Statistics' 2011 American Time Use Survey, **high school students spent on average less than an hour per weekday on sports, exercise and recreation**."[27]

Teens spend <u>more</u> than 7 1 / 2 hours a day consuming media	VS	High school students spent on average <u>less than</u> an hour per weekday on sports, exercise and recreation

Another survey conducted by GfK found:

"The amount of time teens aged 13-17 are spending online

---

[25] http://pediatrics.aappublications.org/content/132/5/958.full

[26] Ibid.

[27] http://www.washingtonpost.com/postlive/teens-are-spending-more-time-consuming-media-on-mobile-devices/2013/03/12/309bb242-8689-11e2-98a3-b3db6b9ac586_story.html

grew by a considerable degree in the space of a year, details GfK in recent survey findings. Results from GfK's Spring 2013 study indicate that **13-17-year-olds spent an average of 4 hours and 4 minutes per day online**, a 37% hike from just under 3 hours per day a year earlier."[28]

"The sizable increase in teens' online time owes mostly to their growing time spent accessing the Internet from tablets (up 157% year-over-year to more than a half-hour per day), smartphones (up 72% to more than one hour per day) and connected TVs (up 86% to 13 minutes per day)."[29]

- Total media usage for teens breakdown – 52.5 hours/week, 210 hours/month, 2520 hours/year

- Online specific breakdown – 30.8 hours/week, 123.2 hours/month, 1478.4 hours/year

What would your student's grades look like if those hours devoted to media, were instead devoted to education or what would your family life look like if this same time was spent on building family relationships?

Is there a problem?

If you want to know if you or a member of your family's Internet/social media/gaming use is a problem, you need to know the warning signs that indicate greater than normal use. Dr. Kimberly Young, Director of the Center for Internet Addiction

---

[28] http://www.gfk.com/us/news-and-events/press-room/press-releases/pages/teens-time-spent-online-grew-37-since-2012.aspx

[29] http://www.marketingcharts.com/online/teens-online-time-surges-exceeds-18-49-demo-39314/

Recovery, has developed the following list of warning signs to help you decide if a digital Internet addiction fits you or your loved one.

Potential warning signs for children with pathological Internet use:

- Loses track of time while online

- Sacrifices needed hours of sleep to spend time online

- Becomes agitated or angry when online time is interrupted

- Checks email several times a day

- Becomes irritable if not allowed access to the Internet

- Spends time online in place of homework or chores

- Prefers to spend time online rather than with friends or family

- Disobeys time limits that have been set for Internet usage

- Lies about amount of time spent online or "sneaks" online when no one is around

- Forms new relationships with people he or she has met online

- Seems preoccupied with getting back online when

away from the computer

- Loses interest in activities that were enjoyable before he or she had online access

- Becomes irritable, moody or depressed when not online[30]

It's not just about the kids

As I mentioned earlier, unlike the past where only the younger generations took part in the newest trend, with social media, parents are just as active online as their children. It is just as important relationally to adults as it is for children to have an online presence. In a 2007 PEW study, Internet use between parents and children were found to be remarkably similar.

"Some 93% of youth are online and 94% of their parents are online...There are several parts of the data in this survey that show that the tech profile of <u>parents and teens often mirror each other</u>. **Parents who use the Internet frequently have teenage children who use the Internet frequently.**"[31]

For parents, social media is just as important of a social network tool as for their children. It provides a venue to give and receive support, hear encouragement and get counsel in all areas of life- whether it be social, emotional or spiritual. It also provides an avenue to stay connected to family, neighbors,

---

[30] http://www.ikeepsafe.org/be-a-pro/balance/too-much-time-online/

[31] http://www.pewInternet.org/2007/10/24/parent-and-teen-Internet-use/

and a network of peers, friends, co-workers, acquaintances, etc. Additionally, it provides a place to go for those struggling with loneliness, allowing virtual peer to peer connections that may be absent in their daily life. Social Media can assist parents in finding help for topics like parenting and marriage, learning or refining skills, making money and providing an outlet to express themselves creatively. A 2015 Pew Study revealed that "More than three-quarters (79%) of parents who use social media agree that they get useful information from their social media networks, including 32% who "strongly agree," a proportion similar to that of all social media users (75%) and non-parents."[32]

Additionally, studies show that parents' use of the Internet is not specific to one site but just like their children, is across the board. Also, more than half of parents view specific platforms and sites several times a day.

"Three-quarters of online parents use Facebook, as do 70% of non-parents. Mothers are more likely to use Facebook than fathers, with 81% of moms and 66% of dads using the platform."[33]

"In addition to Facebook, 28 percent of online parents use Pinterest, while 27 percent use LinkedIn, 25 percent use Instagram and 23 percent use Twitter, the report noted. Moms tend to participate on Facebook, Pinterest and Instagram more than dads, and younger parents are also more likely to have Instagram accounts."[34]

---

32 http://www.pewInternet.org/2015/07/16/parents-and-social-media/

33 Ibid.

34 http://www.usnews.com/news/articles/2015/07/16/most-parents-

Parents are also logging onto social media several times a day and checking in on what's going on in the virtual world around them, with mothers doing so more than fathers. **"Parents on Facebook are especially avid users: 75% log on daily, including 51% who do so several times a day."** "Mothers on Facebook are more likely to check the platform several times a day compared with fathers, 56% vs. 43%."[35]

As you can see, all this accounts for time spent distracted and "elsewhere" or away from other responsibilities. If we are not careful, we run the risk of neglecting our most important tasks. When it comes to social media, it can be a place of great encouragement and support as long as we keep focused and don't lose sight of the world outside of our digital universe.

use-social-media-facebook

35 http://www.pewInternet.org/2015/07/16/parents-and-social-media/

Chapter 4: Email, Texting and Gaming

Another great time waster is email. People have the propensity to check and recheck emails several times a day.

"Email is the biggest time consumer, researchers found. **Respondents said they spend nearly eight hours a week checking emails.**"[36]

Additionally, "**The average person checks email 15 times a day.**"[37]

Most of the times when I check and recheck email--yes I'm guilty of this myself--I find that all that has been added to my inbox is junk, spam or email that I can wait on. Yet while I know this to be true, something within me urges me to check my inbox. Even before I was a stay-at-home mom, I used to check my corporate email several times a day. Interestingly, research is showing that the more you check your email, the more stressed you'll become.

"Checking email may be an addictive habit, but not surprisingly, researchers say the more you refresh your inbox, the more stressed you'll become. According to a study out of the University of British Columbia, there's a cap on the number of times you should check email throughout the day to reduce

---

[36] http://www.businessnewsdaily.com/4718-weekly-online-social-media-time.html#sthash.2ldAoiGi.dpuf

[37] http://mashable.com/2014/12/12/email-checking-study/

stress: three. While the average person checks email 15 times a day, the study suggests three times is the right amount to keep added stress away."[38]

If you are like me, you don't need to check your email more often than three times a day. If you are looking for ways to reduce your stress and have a healthier balanced life, cut down your email viewing to three times a day.

You may also find it helpful to limit how much time you spend responding to emails. This is especially true if you have some sort of leadership or ownership role with people underneath you that are looking for direction, instruction and guidance. Make sure that during those three times a day that you check email, you are not allowing yourself to be consumed by how long you spend responding. If it's possible, delegate some of the emails to others so they can respond for you. Eliminate any email that you don't have to respond to. By doing this, you can also give greater attention to those you do have to respond to.

Texting

I seldom go anywhere without seeing someone texting. It consumes as much time as social media and it definitely stands in its own category of a helpful tool that we need to learn to be self-disciplined with. Like email, texting has diminished or replaced some of the more traditional ways people used to communicate. It has become a primary mode of communication in our culture, especially with teens and young adults.

For many teens, texting is the dominant way that they com-

---

[38] http://mashable.com/2014/12/12/email-checking-study/

municate on a day-to-day basis with their friends.

- **Some 88% of teen's text their friends at least occasionally, and fully 55% do so daily.**[39]

- **51 % of teens who own cellphones use them as their <u>main</u> type of communication.**[40]

This is not necessarily a bad thing. There has been debate as to whether texting makes people less social or instead, provides another avenue for children to keep in contact with their peers by helping them to be more socially interactive with each other. It is easy to see both the positive and negative possibilities that texting provides. Either way you look at texting, it is a major, if not the most predominant communication tool.

In a 2010 Pew study it was noted that, "Two thirds of the testers surveyed by the center's Internet and American Life Project said they were more likely to use their cellphones to text friends than to call them. **Fifty-four percent said they text their friends once a day, but only 33 percent said they talk to their friends face-to-face on a daily basis.**"[41] This study highlighted that more teens text to communicate than engage in face-to-face interaction, which to some people, might give an indication of an emerging problem. However, Rich Ling from PewInternet.org believes the results might indicate an increase in social interaction, not a diminishing of it stating, "Thus, another interpretation is that teens actually

---

[39] http://www.pewInternet.org/2015/08/06/teens-technology-and-friendships/

[40] http://www.alive.com/family/teenagers-and-social-media/

[41] http://www.nytimes.com/2010/05/02/fashion/02BEST.html?_r=0

have more access and more informal, casual contact because of texting. This is because texting is woven into the flow of other activities...Rather than becoming monks sitting in their cells, the material may actually point in the direction of more social interaction, not less."

The question as to how texting is affecting social interaction and normal social growth and development is one that will take years to really understand. Another great question to consider is not just how texting is affecting peer relationships and social development, but whether there can be any quality and depth to a conversation in which one or both parties are texting people at the same time they are talking to one another. To me, that question is far more important. We need to question if we are really actively engaging someone and giving them our full attention, if at the same time we are having and maintaining a separate text based conversation.

How interwoven is texting in children's lives? "More than half of teen texters report texting on a daily basis. In fact, 1 in 3 teens report sending more than 100 messages per day (that's about 3,000 texts a month). **About 15% of teen texters report to sending more than 200 texts a day or 6,000 texts a month!**"[42]

There is no comparison when you consider texting versus any other mode of communication currently in our culture. It is the primary source by which teens choose to interact. When you consider that "63% of all teens say they exchange text messages every day with people in their lives...This far surpasses the frequency with which they pick other forms of dai-

---

[42] https://www.psychologytoday.com/blog/teen-angst/201103/teen-texters

ly communication, including phone calling by cellphone (39% do that with others every day), face-to-face socializing outside of school (35%), social network site messaging (29%), instant messaging (22%), talking on landlines (19%) and emailing (6%)."[43]

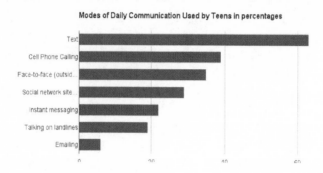

Modes of Daily Communication Used by Teens in percentages

Clearly, texting is a major part of the teen culture. It is helping teens stay more connected to one another, but it may also be hindering social development and affecting face-to-face interaction. Hilary Stout, author of a New York Times article "Antisocial Networking", makes an important observation on the these issues: "Today's youths may be missing out on experiences that help them develop empathy, understand emotional nuances and read social cues like facial expressions and body language."[44]

Kids are learning to hide behind their phones rather than engage in a conversation they can't control. This may have a dramatic impact on their development. As parents, we need to allow them the freedom to text as a means of conversing but

[43] http://www.pewInternet.org/files/old-media/Files/Reports/2012/PIP_Teens_Smartphones_and_Texting.pdf

[44] http://www.nytimes.com/2010/05/02/fashion/02BEST.html

also encourage them to engage in face-to-face interaction with others, even if it makes them feel uncomfortable. This is where wisdom needs to meet culture.

Gaming

The virtual world inhabited by gamers can be more real than the world around them. That is just one of the revelations coming from a new documentary out of China called Web Junkie by Shosh Shlam and Hilla Medalia. The documentary "highlights the tragic effects on teenagers who become hooked on video games, playing for dozens of hours at a time often without breaks to eat, sleep or even use the bath-room."[45]

Can gaming be a real addiction? Consider that people have ac-tually died because of complications due to marathon gaming. Many of them reported using similar phrases before their death that addicts use like "not being able to control it" or "not being able to quit" the game. One particularly sad story I read while doing research for this book involves a Korean couple whose baby, Sarang, died as a result of starvation and neglect because her parents were too busy gaming and ironi-cally, raising a virtual baby together.

 In a 2007 study conducted by Harris Interactive of 1,178 U.S. children and teens (ages 8 to 18) it was found that **nearly 23% of youth report that they feel "addicted to video games" (31% of males, 13% of females.)**[46]

---

[45] http://well.blogs.nytimes.com/2015/07/06/screen-addiction-is-taking-a-toll-on-children/?_r=0

[46] http://www.ikeepsafe.org/be-a-pro/balance/too-much-time-online/

More has to be done to understand the impact and scope of gaming addiction and the health complications from gaming without break, rest, food or movement for hours or days on end.

Violence in games

Virtual worlds allow you to be anyone or do anything without any real (non-virtual) consequences or punishment. Want to kill a cop? Want to rape a woman? Want to have an affair? If so, there's a game out there for you. A lot of games glorify and reward behaviors that would have terrible consequences in the real world. Sometimes circumstances are built in the game itself which punish crimes committed in the virtual world, but the way that violence and crimes are glorified in these games can have the effect of making the players more prone to violent acts in real life.

"**Those who watch a lot of simulated violence, common in many popular video games, can become immune to it, more inclined to act violently themselves and less likely to behave empathetically**", says Dimitri A. Christakis of the Seattle Children's Research Institute."[47]

People are learning not just to take part in violent acts but also subconsciously learning to not have compassion or concern for others. They are training their mind to accept, diminish and embrace activities that are inherently evil and morally wrong. This is a problem.

The mind needs time to imagine and dream

---

[47] http://well.blogs.nytimes.com/2015/07/06/screen-addiction-is-taking-a-toll-on-children/?_r=0

If I allowed my children the opportunity, they would play videogames for countless hours on end, which is why we have game time limitations set up in our house. I notice that after they have played video games for a while, I almost have to retrain their minds to imagine. This is especially true of my seven year old. I will hear phrases like "I'm bored!" and "There is nothing to do!" so I have to encourage them to "find something to do!" They eventually do, of course, but if I allowed them to, they would choose the easiest activity (not always the best) to stimulate their mind. The mind needs time to explore, imagine and dream. Time to think great thoughts, to be inquisitive, to create...inventions, music, works of art, stories, adventures, etc. The author of the best-selling book "The Big Disconnect: Protecting Childhood and Family Relationships in the Digital Age" and Harvard-affiliated clinical psychologist, Dr. Catherine Steiner-Adair, said "If kids are allowed to play 'Candy Crush' on the way to school, the car ride will be quiet, but that's not what kids need," Dr. Dr. Catherine Steiner-Adair said in an interview. "They need time to daydream, deal with anxieties, process their thoughts and share them with parents, who can provide reassurance."

Dr. Steiner-Adair added, "Children have to know that life is fine off the screen. It's interesting and good to be curious about other people, to learn how to listen. It teaches them social and emotional intelligence, which is critical for success in life."[48]

Having time to process life is essential for every human being. Children need to learn that it is okay to be bored and to allow their minds to rest. They need time to not do anything but let thoughts move through their mind unimpeded or interrupted

---

[48] http://well.blogs.nytimes.com/2015/07/06/screen-addiction-is-taking-a-toll-on-children/?_r=0

by entertainment of any sort.

This is true of adults too. My mind is so set on how fast things are these days that I find it increasingly more difficult to concentrate and focus. There was a time I could spend hours focusing on a particular task in detail, but recently, I find myself merely skimming articles or giving a cursory glance to what needs more attention. If you have felt the same way, I have included a fast/detox in Appendix A that I did to help me begin the process of retraining my mind to rest, concentrate and focus.

Video game safety

Another interesting component when considering gaming for our children is safety. Pedophiles look for any way to have direct access and interaction with children, and the digital world provides easy access through social media, forums and gaming. All these platforms give pedophiles contact with our children, and many times both parents and children are unaware of it.

The FBI warns that, "Pedophiles go where children are. Before the Internet, that meant places such as amusement parks and zoos. Today, the virtual world makes it alarmingly simple for pedophiles—often pretending to be teens themselves—to make contact with young people."[49]

While parents are becoming increasingly aware of the danger of pedophiles prowling the Internet, most parents don't consider that gaming is being used as a means for pedophiles to have access to their kids.

---

[49] https://www.fbi.gov/news/stories/2011/may/predators_051711

"Special Agent Wesley Tagtmeyer and other cyber investigators say a relatively new trend among pedophiles is to begin grooming youngsters through online gaming forums, some of which allow two-way voice and video communication. Parents who might be vigilant about monitoring their children's Internet activity often have no idea that online video gaming platforms can pose a threat."[50]

Parents need to consider that if there is any digital means left unprotected or open for a pedophile to gain access to their children, it can be exploited.

They are not all bad

While some individual videogames and excess gaming time are unhealthy for you or your children, video games are not bad, per se. Like anything else, the value is in how you use it. There are many articles and studies showing the benefits that video games offer people. Studies are showing that gaming may help with problems and conditions including: Autism, Multiple Sclerosis (MS), Attention Deficit Disorder (ADD)/Attention Deficit Hyperactivity Disorder (ADHD), educational issues, dyslexia and stress, just to name a few. Gaming together can also be a great way to spend time with your kids and share in their likes and interests.

I'm definitely not a proponent of completely removing gaming. Actually, I play games with my kids on occasion and we all have a great time doing it. I am just mindful of the importance of keeping our times and games limited to things that benefit and strengthen our family.

---

[50] https://www.fbi.gov/news/stories/2011/may/predators_051711

Balance

I try to raise my children with balance. I must remember how important it is to give them autonomy. A child's freedom to choose and make their own decisions becomes vital in their path to adulthood, even if it ends in failure or heartbreak. This is a challenging issue to navigate as a parent; however, if we don't allow them the ability to begin to self-govern and evaluate their world around them, we lead them towards failure. In the end we wind up developing a needy, weak and fearful child instead of an independent, resilient and hopeful child. I always pray to God and affirm to myself that I won't parent in fear and foolishness, but in faith and wisdom.

While the Internet can be a fearful, time consuming place, it can also be a place to teach and train our children in the importance of self-control and self-discipline. As a whole, it is a good place to gently lead them and stay balanced. There are good and necessary tools that social media and the Internet provide daily for my children and my family. I use them every day and I'm thankful for them.

What I am addressing here is the need for knowledge so that you can take back lost time and learn to be more purposeful with the time that you do have. This is also about personal revelation and opening your eyes to see if your family needs change and how to go about that change.

When all's said and done, as long as you can balance the secondary need -- to keep connected to digital resources, with the primary need -- to spend time with your loved ones, you are on the right path. It's all about balance!

Chapter 5: Regaining Time

Let's take back some of that time lost to social media that was uncovered in the last chapter. "New research has found that **the average user spends 23 hours a week emailing, texting and using social media and other forms of online communication**. That number represents **nearly 14 percent of the total time in a week**."[51] If you aren't spending more than 14% of your time devoted to building your marriage, family, friendships, business/career, mind, or character, then things need to change. Below are some ways to help you get there.

Before you start implementing the following ideas, my suggestion is to have a family meeting or discussion and go over a few key elements:

1. **Discuss:** What you have come to realize about the unhealthy Internet use in your house?

2. **Explain the why:** (a) How this use has affected you and/or your family. (b) The negative things you want to see changed. (c) The positive things you want to see strengthened. (Be specific here!)

3. **What you are going to do about it:** Steps that you and your family will take in order to get back in balance and start to regain lost time. (Be sure to be firm here!)

---

[51] http://www.businessnewsdaily.com/4718-weekly-online-social-media-time.html#sthash.2ldAoiGi.dpuf

4. **Why it's important**: This is probably the easiest part of your discussion. The why is because you love them and your relationship with them matters.

5. **What will be gained:** Whenever my husband or I remove or limit something with our family or children, we prefer to highlight what will be gained instead of just highlighting what will be lost. This always helps the sting of losing something treasured and also helps us to stay committed to the change.

6. **Take responsibility:** Whether you do it at the end of your discussion or in another place, personal responsibility needs to be taken for your individual role in the imbalance that has been allowed to develop from Internet use.

Idea 1: Develop overall time limits. If you or your children are normally on the Internet sporadically throughout the day, you will first need to get a clear picture of how much time is being spent online. Afterwards, you can set time limits based on how long you or they are online and how much time you are looking to regain. You can use the television time savings breakdown from my first chapter on television use to give you an idea of how much Internet use needs to be limited, based on how much time you are looking to regain or how much of a problem the current Internet use is.

Idea 2: Set usage hours. You can easily bypass all the number crunching by setting definitive time hour limits. For example, Internet use is allowed only between the hours of 6-8 p.m. Many popular wireless routers on the market support time based access/restriction features that will make this an easily enforced policy.

Idea 3: Make usage reward or merit based. Grant use based on a reward or merit based system. Rewards can be given for good behavior, grades, chores, or anything else you decide. You can even combine this with **Idea 2** and have set Internet use hours that are given daily and extra time can be earned only through reward. We've done merit based use in different ways in our family. For example, in addition to rewarding good behavior, good grades and completing chores, we have also implemented that each minute reading earns the same time online. Each book read earns a specific amount of screen time. Godly character (outside of good behavior) can earn time. These are just a few ways to use this idea.

Idea 4: Only go online in the morning and the evening. This is something that I suggest specifically to moms. Check your email and look online in the morning before your children wake up and then look at it in the evening, once your children have gone to bed and your day is coming to a close. This way you do not neglect your children, your family or your responsibilities.

Idea 5: Time limiting apps/software. Purchase time limiting apps or software. This is not meant to be an enforcer, but for accountability. With anything else, what you use is not as important as your commitment to abide by it. Many of the apps and time limitation software have an administrative bypass to them. In order to make these time limiting options work, you need to be committed to using them.

Idea 6: No television or Internet connected devices in kids' rooms. There is no way you can fully police or monitor the time or the content of your children's Internet/social media/television use if it is in their room. This is a suggestion also recommended by the American Academy of Pediatrics.[52]

Idea 7: Spend family time "disconnected." Require that all purposeful family time be completely device free. This is self-explanatory. Exceptions can be made for long vacations or travel with moderation.

Being Purposeful

Of all the good things to pursue, the one with the greatest and longest return is spending time with your family. With purposeful family building times, there should be **NO** electronic media or distractions allowed. A note on not allowing electronic media of any kind is needed here. This will be something that people will rebel with at first, but in time it will be understood and accepted as the new norm. The time together must be free from anything that would distract from family building time. Unless there is an emergency, everything else can wait and should be secondary to time spent together.

Here are some ways to make lasting memories and regain and recapture lost time.

Suggestion 1: Family Game Nights. This can be any sort of fun game to help build and strengthen your family bond. It can be board games, card games or interactive games like hide and seek, Nerf gun/water balloon battles, kick the can, etc. The game should be something everyone can take part in and there should be no electronic media or distractions allowed. When we are playing a game where our littlest children are too young to participate, we always find a way to incorporate them. Sometimes that's only done by having them "be on our

---

[52] http://pediatrics.aappublications.org/content/132/5/958.full

teams" or be our helpers. Usually we make a dessert for the night or make homemade popcorn. We do our best to make these moments special, especially for our children. Playing family games builds qualities like honesty, togetherness, self-control, instruction, patience, problem solving and good sportsmanship. In our house, we always look forward to game nights.

Suggestion 2: Family Dinner. Thirty years ago I might not have had to include a suggestion for family dinners but unfortunately it is necessary today. Eating together as a family builds qualities like intimacy, encouragement, support, unity, understanding and communication. The dinner table is a place where you can laugh, cry, yell and encourage the people who love you and know you the best. It's about being together and being a part of one another's world. The dinner table should be a place of honesty and grace.

One of the fun things we like to do at the dinner table is Table Fun Questions. We have a bunch of questions in a large size mason jar and we all go around the table and each person asks a question and we all answer them. We don't always do this but when we do, we really enjoy it. I love the questions because they can be a real avenue for you to get to know your family more intimately. This is not my idea originally, but I have made up my own questions along the way and tailored others to suit our family. I have created over 200 of them in Appendix B, found at the back of this book, with directions on how to structure this time. This is my free gift to you, to help you build a stronger family.

Suggestion 3: Family Devotions. As a Christian, family devotions are extremely important in our house. We have them together as a family or in smaller groups within our family (whole family; husband and wife; parent and child; child and child) depending on the situation or need. It is an area where we grow spiritually as a family and individually. It is also a place where we get to know each other deeper and where we can pray for each other and our needs. It is an excellent practice to have and will strengthen your family bond in ways that normal time together will not. Having family devotions builds characteristics like love, togetherness, spiritual/emotional strength, instruction, correction, selflessness, perseverance and responsibility. I believe every positive family characteristic is built through family devotions. There are some great resources online to help you get started and you are welcome to email me if you need a little help along the way. You can always start by just reading the Bible and discussing it.

Suggestion 4: Hiking. We love to hike together as a family. We have hiked parts of the Appalachian Trail, C & O Railroad, some small mountains, state parks, nature trails, reservoirs and other places. My kids all carry a backpack when we hike and we all get walking sticks. We usually pack lunches and snacks and we set off on a mini adventure in the woods. Hiking builds qualities like perseverance, adventure, togetherness, love and respect of nature, strength, hard work, leadership, selflessness and responsibility. When we are done and get back to our starting point, everyone has such a sense of accomplishment. There's so much beauty you see in nature when you go hiking. The world slows down for a while and you can appreciate all of God's beautiful creation. There's a lot that hiking is good for as a family and it definitely works on building the family unit. I have had many great talks with my children and husband on hikes.

Suggestion 5: Make and follow a family fun bucket list. I love making bucket lists. We do one for every season and when the year ends, we place it in a memory jar or family time capsule with some other things we gathered from the year's activities. We also usually place an end of year family picture in the jar and funny stories and quotes/sayings we might have said throughout the year. The bucket list helps to keep our family accountable with how much time we spend together strengthening the family bond. It also helps to be purposeful as a family with our time together. In the past I have chosen certain things from our bucket list and put it on our calendar to ensure it gets done. Making family bucket lists builds a desire for family time, fun, accountability, discipline and love into your family life. I created some free family bucket list documents for you to fill out. You can find these and other free resources at LoraZiebro.com.

Suggestion 6: Cook Together. I love cooking with my kids. When we cook and bake together, I don't stress about how the kitchen looks. I am a recipe kind of mom so my kids have learned how to follow recipes well. They really feel a sense of accomplishment when they are done and the food tastes great. We always make sure that we thank that night's chef for their tasty meal. My kids will even prepare dinners on their own sometimes. Cooking together as a family builds qualities like service, following instruction, selflessness, responsibility, problem solving and being thorough. It's an excellent activity to do together as a family.

Suggestion 7: Family Sports. We love a good kickball game at our house. We play sports together a lot as a family. We usually play kickball because even our youngest can participate-- but we will also play football, soccer, volleyball, basketball and baseball on occasion. Sometimes we just throw the ball around and play catch. Playing sports together as a family is a great way to spend time together. Playing family sports builds qualities like team building, patience, self-control, integrity, leadership, healthy competition and good sportsmanship. It is a great family activity for the whole family.

Suggestion 8: Family movie night. As you can tell from my first chapter, I'm not a big proponent of watching television;

however, I love family movie nights in our house. We all get together, grab blankets and snuggle down with each other and eat popcorn or ice cream. We choose different types of wholesome movies. Many times, my husband and I use the plot to talk about serious or important issues going on around us. Watching good family movies can teach/show everything from honor, courage, loyalty, humor, love and leadership, to negative consequences as a result of bad decisions. Watching television as a family where you are all physically close to each other can really be a special moment in your family week. As long as being together as a family is the primary focus, a good movie can be a wonderful activity for the whole family.

Suggestion 9: Going on walks. I love to go on walks with my family. Sometimes it's all of us and sometimes I'll just go on a walk with one of my children to have a good heart-to-heart or mother-child moment with them. It depends on the situation. It is an activity that can be done daily and is good for your overall mental, physical and spiritual health. We love to go out as the day is starting to cool off a bit and just walk around and talk. We hold hands, we jump around, we look at bugs or animals, do nature scavenger hunts, catch fireflies, etc. It's such a tranquil time for us as a family. Because I have five children, tranquility is something that is a treasured and rare commodity in our home. Going on walks with your family builds qualities like peacefulness, togetherness, communication, love and respect of nature and thoughtfulness.

Suggestion 10: Exercising Together. My husband and I like to live a healthy lifestyle. Overall we eat really healthy and we both like to exercise. Many times we have our kids with us when we exercise, depending on what we are doing. We run, walk and bike and do strength training with our kids. I love when I'm doing a particular exercise and I see my little daughter next to me trying to do what I am doing. It's such a cute moment. Many times, good health is learned from parents, as is bad health. Exercise is such a good activity for your overall health. It can help with problems like anxiety, stress and depression and offers a healthier way to handle difficulties than taking up a negative vice to relieve your problems. Exercising teaches characteristics like self-control, discipline, focus, diligence, hard work, perseverance and strength.

Suggestion 11: Serving Together. Serving others is such a great way to teach your family to have a heart for people. It helps them look outside of themselves and their needs and has them focus on someone else's. It also helps develop essential heart qualities in your family- qualities like selflessness, kindness, empathy, appreciation, compassion, giving and love. It has been said that a great way to get over or look past your own problems is to help another person with theirs. There's something powerful about getting the focus off of us and putting it on another person. It also is a good way to show your family just how fortunate they are. There are so many good organizations and places to serve. You can volunteer at homeless shelters, youth related events, inner city clubs, special needs organizations, churches, pregnancy centers, or nursing homes. You can help elderly, widowed or sickly neighbors with chores around their house. You can make cookies or food for the local fire or police department or go on mission trips in America or internationally. There are so many good ways to help and serve your community and teach your family to have a heart that cares for others.

Suggestion 12: Build something or work on something together. I come from a long line of people who like working with their hands. We create, build, shape and labor with our hands and we love it. Over the years my husband and I have started to pass on this love to our children. My dad is also a great influence in this area. He loves to show my children how to work with their hands and they love to listen and learn from him. There is something very special and unique about learning a trade that has been passed down from one generation to another. My family also loves to learn new skills and trades. We may not know how to do something but we all work together and figure it out along the way. Creating something, working together on a project or building together are great ways to strengthen your family and spend time together. It is also important to show your children the skills that make your family interesting or unique, as in a special ability or trade. When you as a family build, create or complete a project together, there is a real sense of unity and accomplishment. It teaches qualities like problem solving, unity, hard work, responsibility, diligence, sweat equity, patience and perseverance. It's a great family bonding activity.

Suggestion 13: Family Outdoor Fun. There are endless activities you can do as a family outdoors. There are activities that are just for fun; ones that can help children take personal ownership and have a greater sense of purpose in their home; those directly outside the home that you don't have to go anywhere for; and activities that you can do on a family field trip.

Being outdoors helps to unplug from the digital world and helps us appreciate the beauty of the world around us. It helps strengthen the family unit and builds qualities like ownership, responsibility, togetherness, hard work, good sportsmanship, healthy competition, tranquility, patience, adventure and love of nature. There are so many great things to do and learn outside.

Here is a short list of fun or wholesome family outdoor activities.

1. Catch fireflies

2. Pitch and sleep outdoors in a tent

3. Build and tend to a flower or vegetable garden

4. Make and use a slip and slide

5. Water gun/balloon fights

6. Nerf battles

7. Star gazing and identification

8. Swimming

9. Roast marshmallows, hot dogs or make s'mores around a fire

10. Bike rides

11. Yard maintenance

12. Nature scavenger hunt

13. Throw rocks in a creek or stream

14. Have a family picnic

15. Go to a park

16. Go to a farm. Many farms teach courses like bee keeping, gardening, and many others!

17. Go to a playground or play on a playset at home

18. Jump on a trampoline if you have one – remember

safety first!

19. Nature (plant, animal, bird, insect) identification

20. Cloud watching

21. Sports

22. Build a treehouse

23. Obstacle course – go to a tree climbing or obstacle course or create one in your backyard

24. Vegetable/fruit picking by season – loads of fun and you can bake a pie with what you pick

25. Nature (survival) courses, usually found at local or state parks – some courses offered around us are: learning to build a fire, purify water, and plant identification

26. Go play miniature golf or create one in your backyard

27. Just go outside walking and enjoy the outdoors

Additionally, if you have a child with ADD or ADHD, studies show outdoor "green" time is very important and helpful to them. My son benefits greatly from being outside. It helps him with focus and it refreshes his spirit.

Suggestion 14: Art /Craft/Science fun. My kids love to do art and craft projects or science experiments together. It's a great creative way to spend time together as a family. We paint, design jewelry, make decorations, work on different experiments, and color. We have even created things to sell! I get ideas from places like Pinterest, art/craft/science books and free teacher resources online. Sometimes we just wing it and see what we can create together.

Additionally, I also like to redesign and flip furniture and work on wood to sell. I love to have my kids join in. Working together on artistic, creative projects teaches qualities like love of art, personal excellence, problem solving, unity, hard work, diligence, sweat equity, and patience.

Suggestion 16: Clean/Do Household Chores Together. There are a lot of benefits that cleaning together provides for a family. It is a great opportunity to train your children to care for their house, their family and their environment. It is a great opportunity to correct bad character traits and reinforce good ones. For example, if you have a child who struggles with laziness or follow through, it is a great way to teach hard work and perseverance. We usually put on music and everyone has an area of responsibility with some children sharing areas of responsibility.

I'm not big about allowing a label to define my child, especially in a negative way. One of my children has ADD. When he works with us I try to use that time to teach him and work with him on and through his focus issues. I will help give him tools to do a better job and work more efficiently.

One of the tools I have used is to help him compartmentalize his chores. This is very difficult for him to do on his own. For example, where you might tell a child to "go clean your room", I need to compartmentalize (break down) that chore for my son to help him be successful. Instead I'll have to say:

Bedroom

- Separate clothes on floor

- Put dirty clothes in hamper

- Put clean clothes away

  1. Clothes that should be hung up, hang up

  2. Clothes that should be folded, fold

- Pick up everything off the floor. Pay special attention to corners, behind door and under bed

- Put away toys and books neatly where they belong

- Dust and clean dresser

- Change pillow cases and sheets if needed, make bed when done

- Pick up any garbage and put it in the garbage can

- Vacuum floor

- Double check work

I will give him this list on a laminated piece of paper or small white board for him to check off tasks as he completes them. This helps him to stay focused as well as encourages him as he completes chores and checks off his tasks.

I have created an example chore chart that I use. You can find this and other free resources at LoraZiebro.com. Working/Doing chores together teaches qualities like hard work, discipline, responsibility, diligence, and perseverance.

Suggestion 17: Name game/Rhyming game. This is a fun game we play on car trips. It's a great way to have fun and spend time together.

Name Game – Someone starts off the game with a name. The last letter of that name is the first letter of the next name. The next player must start the name with the last letter. So if I said Steven, The next player would have to say a name that starts with "N". This process continues with the next player and so on. It continues until someone repeats or can't think of a name in enough time (usually 30 seconds). If either occurs, that person is out until the next game. We play until there's one person left who wins the game. We play this using U.S. Capitals, cities and states too. Sometimes we will have a name theme like superheroes which is always fun for my kids. To include my little non-spellers, I just let them say any name they can think of.

Rhyming Game – Someone starts off the game with a word. Everyone has a turn to find a word that rhymes until a person can't think of one. This person is then out and you continue until there's a winner. Example – 1st player starts with the word "time," 2nd player says "rhyme," 3rd player says "chime," etc.

There are many different fun or educational type games you can choose as a way to spend time together with our family. They teach qualities like problem solving, unity, patience, good sportsmanship and healthy competition.

Suggestion 18: Dance/sing with your kids. I love to dance and sing with my kids. I don't have a great voice but when we are singing and dancing, my kids don't mind. This is always a fun time for us. Sometimes we sing songs we know; sometimes we make up crazy songs or give songs that we do know, crazy lyrics. It doesn't matter as long as we are having fun.

I have taught my boys how to dance with a girl, how to keep a beat, how to breakdance (a little) and how to two-step. They have a confidence in dancing they wouldn't have had outside of these awesome times of fun. Singing and dancing with your kids builds qualities like courage (for the shy type, it gets them out of their shell), spontaneity, patience, perseverance, focus, self-control and togetherness.

Suggestion 19: Read to your kids. One of the best ways to spend quality time with your children is to read books to them or have them read to you. The benefits of reading to them offer more than just the intimate development one on one time achieves. There is a profound effect reading has on the intellectual development of your child. The British Cohort Study has been observing 17,000 people over the course of their life span and how reading played an effect on their life. It observed the intellectual increase reading played in their development- specifically, math, vocabulary, and spelling.[53]

"Perhaps surprisingly, reading for pleasure was found to be more important for children's cognitive development between ages 10 and 16 than their parents' level of education. The combined effect on children's progress of reading books often, going to the library regularly and reading newspapers at 16 was four times greater than the advantage children gained from having a parent with a degree. Children who were read to regularly by their parents at age 5 performed

---

[53]

http://www.cls.ioe.ac.uk/page.aspx?&sitesectionid=795&sitesectiontitle=Welcome+to+the+1970+British+Cohort+Study

better in all three tests at age 16 than those who were not helped in this way."[54]

Reading is extremely important to a child's intellectual development as the study shows but the simple act of a parent reading to his or her child has far more impact than just intellectual development. There is a personal and intimate connection that comes from spending that time with your child. As you read together, you both enter a world of adventure, history, intrigue and excitement. Reading is a far greater use of time, and the enjoyment is felt on both sides. Plus, if you have a library card, the cost of the fun is free. You can't beat that!

As a side note, in our home I am purposeful with the books I select to read to my children personally or have them read individually. If they are not reading for a school assignment, I look for books that help develop character, encourage personal growth, show courage, teach something new, develop wonder and adventure and strengthen the spirit. My children also have a time of free reading where they can choose to read anything they want. Even then, I try to encourage them to make good choices. Unfortunately, too many books these days offer nothing worthy of the time spent reading them.

Suggestion 20: Make up and tell stories together. A fun alternative to reading that we like to do in our family is to make up stories together. It is a great variation to reading together. Usually one of us will start and tell his portion of the story until he has nothing more to say--or he will purposefully stop in a suspenseful place. Another family member picks up where he left off and we continue like that until the story goes to its gradual end. Sometimes one of us will just tell a story until

---

[54] http://www.ioe.ac.uk/89938.html

completion. I do this a lot with my kids at bedtime. Our stories are sometimes magical, sometimes suspenseful, many times funny and silly and always a good time for everyone. It's a great creative outlet and helps them educationally as well. I always make my kids the heroes of the tales. It's a great way to speak life and value into them and let them see what I see within them as a person.

Remember, the key is to focus on the experience and the time spent together!

What's the point?

When people near the end of their life, many times there's a lot of deep reflection and contemplation and regret on the roads they did take, the roads they didn't take and the ones they wished they had gone down. No one wishes they made more money; no one wishes they spent more time online or on their smartphone; no one wishes they pinned more recipes or crafts; or liked more posts, or watched more YouTube videos. People wish they spent more time with those they love. They wish they made more of an eternal and personal impact on their family, in this world and the next. They look and long for the regaining of their precious time lost on things that mattered so little. Lost time is one of the biggest regrets people have in the end and one they wish they could change. Our truest and best legacy will not be about any of the things that are fleeting. It will be defined the greatest by those who we have invested our lives into, in a deep, intimate way. The Bible says, "Let the wise hear and increase in learning, and the one who understands obtain guidance" Proverbs 1:5. My hope, my prayer, is that you set out to develop a legacy that matters to those who, at night, will close their eyes and remember you when all the rest of the world has forgotten.

Today can be different!

ABOUT LORA

Lora Ziebro is a mom of 5 wonderfully loud and awesome children. Two of her children have special needs (Down Syndrome and developmental delays), and several have ADD/ADHD. Additionally, one of her son's has Tourette's syndrome. Her oldest son and husband has several food related complications that have required her to learn and adapt a healthy, clean, probiotic-rich, family diet. She has been homeschooling her children for 10 years and also teaches logic and apologetics to local middle school and high school children. Lora loves being a mom and a wife, and doing it well is something she constantly strives towards.

Lora has been married to her husband Tom for 14 years now. They met in the U.S. Army and since that one meeting, everything in their lives has interwoven into a beautiful, fun adventure. Tom is her best friend and her greatest confidant.

Lora had worked professionally as a stockbroker, receiving her Series 7 and 63 licenses at 18 years old, followed by a term of service in the U.S. Army where she was an intelligence analyst. She later worked in the private sector as a contracted intelligence analyst in support of the government.

Lora loves interior design and fashion. She also loves working with her hands and is constantly finding old, forgotten pieces of furniture or other items and either reinventing or breathing new life into them. She loves everything vintage, antique and rustic.

Lora loves to help strengthen families and help women grow spiritually, emotionally, professionally and personally. She loves to be a voice of good and hope in the lives of the women she knows. She also loves to teach and speak to women. She is loud, authentic, honest and down to earth.

Lora's greatest love above all things, is Jesus. She accounts anything worth knowing or good about her, due to His grace in her life.

Why she wrote Digital Addiction

Lora wrote this book after going to dinner one night and noticing that almost everyone around her were on their cell phones. She noticed how no one seemed to be having real interaction with each other and she recognized this same problem was present at times in her own life. She recognized the need for a book that didn't just inform but also helped families get stronger.

APPENDIX A

The 30 Day Digital Detox

Whenever anything in my life gets out of order or out of balance, or I start to "need" something that isn't a true necessity, I undertake a 30 day detox or fast from that particular thing. These fasts help me rebalance a particular area in my life. The Bible says **"for by what a man is overcome, by this he is enslaved"** (2 Peter 2:19b). When an activity does become too much for me, I am purposeful to remove its hold over my life. By doing a complete fast, it severs the control that activity has on me.

Afterwards I start to slowly reintroduce the activity in my life (unless it's something I should completely sever) and put in place disciplines and limits to prevent my life from coming under its control again. I also try to understand and fill the underlying need (boredom or laziness) that put me in the place of bondage in the first place, with something healthy and good. <u>Replacing something that is bad or unhealthy with something that is good and healthy is the underlying principle for freedom from any bondage</u>.

The 30 day fast is pretty simple to do. Identify the area of your life that has become out of control and then remove it for 30 days. Pretty straight forward!

The following is the format of a detox/fast I did earlier this year. It is unlike others I've done in that it wasn't done to eliminate a stronghold or vice in my life, but to improve an area I needed to work on. The principles are still the same. I decided to include this particular one because I feel many people struggle with the same problems as me which are neg-

73

ative side effects of this digital age.

Personally, I recognized that I had a hard time slowing down my mind. It was becoming very difficult to read for quality and to concentrate without breezing through or just browsing what I was reading. This was especially true if I was reading something online. I would find an article, breeze through the text (possibly only reading the beginning and last sentences of a paragraph- enough to get the gist) and then finish. When I realized that it was becoming more and more difficult for me to concentrate, I decided to find a solution to retrain my mind.

Here is a summary of the daily steps, principles and techniques that I followed during the process.

1. Implement a total digital media fast. This includes any and all non-essential media devices and communications.

2. Print out articles to read instead of reading them online. There should be no reading on any digital media platform.

3. Find an activity that slows down the brain and forces it to concentrate. Do that activity daily. i.e. a puzzle, a craft/project that requires detail or concentration, or memorization verses.

4. Be deliberate in your efforts to force your brain to concentrate. Purposefully read slower, read the entire article, and maybe even take notes. Write slower- be more intentional.

5. Accountability - Find people to help you and/or hold you accountable.

6. Boredom periods - Allow periods of boredom because they are great for your mind.

7. Set up barriers to prevent falling back into the same place. You can implement the following:

- Time limits

- Website blocks

- Complete removal of any direct access to a particular vice

- Complete removal of any indirect access to a particular vice

- Make the vice as unpleasant as possible. An alternative to a complete removal is to make the access and/or enjoyment to the vice uncomfortable. For example, if television is your vice and you are not able to move it completely from your direct/indirect contact, move the television to an uncomfortable place. Remove it from being in front of a comfortable couch and put it in front of an uncomfortable chair or in a cold room, or a room with no seating at all. Make the experience unpleasant and it will greatly help to diminish the desire to engage in it.

- F. Develop a battle plan. Make a plan that covers "what to do in case of" scenarios and how to successfully navigate them, should they actually occur. These strategies and techniques should be developed, and most importantly, decided upon prior to the temptation of the vice. If you make a firm resolution/self-commitment prior to the temptation, you are far more likely to stick to it. You will find your resolve weaker if you haven't already decided what you will do in case the vice presents itself.

- G. Most importantly, don't allow yourself any excuses. **Not even one!** Either decide to do it or don't waste your time. The choice to change starts first with the will then it's followed by action.

Here are some basic principles to help you be successful

- Find your "why". In order for most people to let go of strongly held vices, their "why" (the reason why they are quitting) has to be stronger than their need for the vice. This is why a person can finally let go of something like smoking when their doctor informs them it's causing lung cancer. Finding and knowing your "why" will enable you to be successful when other things have previously failed.

- Have an accountability partner(s). Select someone to share your struggle with who will help you in your fast. Preferably, someone who has already successfully dealt with the same or a similar struggle in their own life. They will help to keep you accountable and encourage or exhort you if necessary. This person should be faithful and honest enough to say the hard things if needed. They also should not be a person who will allow you to get away with compromise.

- I realize in regard to email, the Internet and texting, there are jobs and activities in our lives that may necessitate being on-line. In those circumstances, fast from **all** non-work and non-essential related use for 30 days. In consideration of friends who may be trying to reach you, you could set up an auto-reply telling them that you will not be checking email until a certain date.

- When thinking about reintroducing an activity, sometimes it's important to ask ourselves questions to evaluate whether or not an activity should be reintroduced.

Ask yourself:

Do your activities help to build relationships with those who matter most to you?

Do your activities make you neglect your primary responsibilities?

Does your involvement in them make your family feel more or less loved? More or less focused on?

Do these activities build you up as a person? Make you a better man/woman?

Could time be spent on better things?

When you do reintroduce the activity, put tools, limitations and disciplines in place to ensure healthy use of the activity and continued success from overuse and waste.

APPENDIX B

Table Talk Fun

Directions for use: Cut each question out separately and place in a jar or can. Read at family meal times or family "together" moments. Some of the questions are deeper and more important than others and are meant to spark weightier conversations, others are light and funny. Either way you will get to know one another better through these questions.

1. What do you think came first, the chicken or the egg, and why?

2. What super power would you rather have, invisibility or indestructibility, and why?

3. Do you think a tree makes a sound if it falls in the forest but no one is around to hear it?

4. What's your favorite color?

5. What's your favorite song?

6. What's your favorite season?

7. What superhero are you most like?

8. What super villain are you most like?

9. What comic book character has the coolest power and why?

10. What's your favorite childhood memory and why?

11. What's your favorite memory with your mom and why?

12. What's your favorite memory with your dad and why?

13. Rap or rock and roll?

14. If someone wanted to create a reality show based on your life, what would the title be?

15. What party do you most identify with Democrat, Republican, Libertarian or none of the above?

16. Which author has written better scary stories Steven King or Edgar Allen Poe?

17. Which of the these three writers do you like better and why- J.K. Rawlings, C.S. Lewis or J.R.R. Tolkien?

18. What's your most embarrassing moment?

19. What's your most victorious moment?

20. What is your favorite music genre?

21. What's your favorite/least favorite food?

22. You are happiest when...?

23. You are saddest when...?

24. Who do you think would win in a fight, a werewolf or a zombie, and why?

25. Who do you think would win in a fight, a lion or a bear?

26. What's the one thing you think you do the best?

27. Would you rather be famous or infamous?

28. What figure in history do you think you are most like?

29. What figure in history would you most like to meet and why?

30. It hurts you when I...?

31. You love when I...?

32. Socks or barefeet?

33. Do you believe in aliens and why?

34. Do you believe in the Lockness Monster or not, and why?

35. Do you believe in Bigfoot or not, and why?

36. Who is one historical figure that you would want to go back in time and visit to show them how their decisions affected mankind? What would you say to help them change their decisions?

37. McDonald's, Wendy's or Burger King?

38. What's one thing about you that you wish you could change?

39. What's one thing about me you wish you could change?

40. What do you want to be when you grow up?

41. What's one decision you wish you could change?

42. Who is your favorite president and why?

43. Beach or mountains?

44. Boat or plane?

45. What's your biggest fear?

46. What teacher has most influenced you and why?

47. What's the one thing you want to accomplish or do before you die?

48. Mustang or Camaro?

49. What's your favorite movie?

50. If you could be on any reality show, what would you be on, and why?

51. You most like when I tell you...?

52. You dislike when I say/do...?

53. Do you prefer mornings or evenings?

54. Do you prefer coffee or tea?

55. Do you prefer ice cream, cookies or cake?

56. Which are cooler, dogs or cats, and why?

57. What bug do you most hate?

58. If for a whole day everything was free, what would you do/"buy"?

59. What's your favorite family memory from this year? From all time?

60. If you could have any creature as a pet, mythical or real, what would you have?

61. Would you rather have trust, love or respect in a relationship?

62. What's your idea of a fun thing to do?

63. What do you think the world will be like in 100 years?

64. Who do you think would win in a fight, Thor or Hulk, and why?

65. What animals or insects are you afraid of?

66. If you could change the world, for good or for bad, what would you do, and why?

67. What's your fist thought when you wake up? What's your last thought before you go to bed?

68. What would be your dream vacation?

69. If you had the power to eradicate only one disease, which would you choose to get rid of?

70. If you could speak with one important person, dead or alive, who would it be, and why?

71. What food would you never eat again for dinner, if you had the choice?

72. What do you feel is the greatest invention of the last 100 years and why?

73. What do you feel is the most dangerous or destructive invention of all time?

74. Do you ever have the same dream over and over again? If so what is it?

75. If you could put hair anywhere on a shark, where would you put it, and why?

76. Do you believe in miracles?

77. What color best describes your personality?

78. What would be worse, an eternity in fire, an eternity alone, or an eternity freezing?

79. What do you think is the scariest way to die?

80. If you could be anything in the world, what would you be?

81. What's the best gift you ever received?

82. If you could go anywhere in the world, where would you go?

83. If you could live in any era, what era would you choose, and why?

84. If you could visit and meet the people of any past civilization, who would you meet?

85. Who do you think you are most like and why?

86. If you could marry any celebrity, who would you marry?

87. What animal would look the weirdest if they had a tiny head? Why?

88. Is there anything you pretend you understand but you really don't?

89. Which one of your friends do you trust the most/least and why?

90. Which one of your friends do you think would take a bullet for you and why?

91. If you could ask God one question, what would it be?

92. If you could take an expedition into deep space, not knowing if you'd return or what you would find, would you do it?

93. What's your favorite and least favorite season and why?

94. What's one thing that I don't allow you to do, that you wish I did?

95. If a genie would grant you any wish (outside of more

wishes), what would it be?

96. What animal do you think is the weirdest and why?

97. What kinds of lies do your friends tell their parents?

98. Do you have many friends?

99. Have you ever been in love?

100. Who do you think is the funniest person in our family?

101. Who do you think is the smartest person in our family?

102. Who do you think is the biggest troublemaker in our family?

103. If you could write a book about anything, what would you write about?

104. Have I ever given you a punishment that you thought was really unfair? If so, what was it? Why do you think it was unfair?

105. If you could be any animal in the world for a day, what would you be, and why?

106. If you could be any famous person in the world for a day, who would you be, and why?

107. What traditions do you most look forward to at family get togethers?

108. What traditions would you like us to start/stop?

109. Which one of your friends (including our family) do you think has the strictest parents? What about them makes them strict? What do you like about that? What would you change?

110. How would you define success?

111. What cartoon character are you most like?

112. What habit that you have or thing that you do would be the hardest to change or break? Would you be willing to change or break it for $1,000,000?

113. What is your most loved or most important possession?

114. What two celebrities do you think should date, and why?

115. What is the craziest or wildest thing you have ever done?

116. What is the scariest thing you have ever done?

117. What is the most important thing you have ever done?

118. What wouldn't you do for all the money in the world?

119. What animal would look the weirdest without eyes? Why?

120. What is the greatest contribution you have made to this world so far?

121. If you could change something about yourself what would it be?

122. What would you say makes a person rich?

123. Do you think there is a difference between being rich and being wealthy, and if so, what would that difference be?

124. What's the most important thing you have learned from your parents?

125. What's the best thing you have learned from your parents? What's the worst?

126. What's the best thing you learned from your sibling(s)?

127. If you could change your name to anything, what would you change it to?

128. Do you think it's better to be liked or to be respected?

129. What do you like most about school? What do you like least?

130. Who is your favorite relative outside of our immediate family?

131. What do you love the most about your family?

132. Look at each member of your family and tell them what you love or like most about them.

133. What would be your dream job or life?

134. Do you feel that you make me proud? Why or why not?

135. What do you think eternity is like?

136. What was your favorite birthday and why?

137. In what ways do you feel most loved?

138. What do I do that makes you feel loved?

139. What is/was your favorite activity to do with your mom/dad?

140. How do you describe your parents to your friends?

141. What gets you the most frustrated?

142. What do you think makes a family, a family?

143. What things/situations gets you the most angry and why?

144. Who do you most want to be like in your family?

145. Do you ever feel lost or alone?

146. What action hero would look best with a mullet – Bruce Willis, the Rock or Vin Diesel?

147. Do you ever feel like a failure? What makes you feel that way? Do I ever contribute to that feeling?

148. What qualities do you think makes someone a good/bad friend?

149. How do you most want to be remembered when you die?

150. If your house was on fire and you could only grab one thing, what would you grab? If everyone was safe, what would you grab?

151. What chore do you hate doing the most?

152. What's one thing you would change about me?

153. When was the best time of your life? What made it the best?

154. If you could meet any world leader today, who would you meet and what would you say to them?

155. What do you think heaven is like?

156. What do I do or say that makes you feel special?

157. Has anyone ever told you to keep a secret from me but you really want to tell me? Would you like to tell me now?

158. Is there something you have wanted to say to me but don't know how to? Would you like to try now?

159. Has anyone ever hurt you but you haven't told me? Would you like to tell me now?

160. Is there any adult you know that makes you feel uncomfortable? What about them makes you feel uncomfortable?

161. Is there anything I do that embarrasses you or makes you feel uncomfortable? Would you like to tell me what it is?

162. What do you think God is like?

163. What do you think makes something true? What do you think makes something false? Do you think those things (what's true and what's false) are governed by feelings or facts?

164. Do you think there is a difference between truth and opinion?

165. What do you think makes a man, a man? A woman, a woman?

166. What do you think makes someone a hero?

167. Would you rather be famous or a hero? Why?

168. Do you think that some conspiracies theories are true?

169. What do you think love is? How would you describe being in love or what makes someone in love? Do you think love is a feeling or a choice?

170. Are there things in school you are taught that you disagree with or upsets you? What are they?

171. What's one hobby you'd like to try?

172. What's one sport you'd like to try?

173. What sayings that I always say drive you crazy?

174. Does it bother you when parents don't apologize and why?

175. What's one thing I tell you to do that you don't feel I do myself? Does that bother you?

176. What family vacation do you want to go on next?

177. Is your heart hurting about anything?

178. What sport that you like to go and see but hate to watch on TV?

179. What's one thing you want me to teach you to do?

180. What's one thing you wish you knew how to do better?

181. What responsibility do you think you are ready for?

182. You don't like that I...?

183. You love that I...?

184. What's one thing that you hate the smell of?

185. Pick any animal and give its "call" an accent? Make it for everyone.

186. What animal would look the weirdest without a nose? Why?

187. What animal do you think has the coolest abilities?

188. If you could time travel just once, would you visit the past or the future and why?

189. It hurts you when I say...?

190. What would you rather come across in the wild, an alligator or a bear, and why?

191. What's one thing I do that you think is pretty cool?

192. What do you like about me over your friend's mom/dad?

193. If you could learn any trade, what would you learn?

194. What do you think makes a person honorable?

195. What are the characteristics of a person with integrity?

196. What are the characteristics of a good leader? Bad leader?

197. What makes a person hard working?

198. Would you rather be bitten by a shark or stung by a box jellyfish?

199. What makes someone disabled?

200. What's one disability you are glad you don't have? Why?

Made in the USA
Middletown, DE
21 November 2017